COLORS OF
Paris

AA Publishing

Author: Mike Gerrard

Produced by AA Publishing

Text © Automobile Association Developments Limited 2004

Published by AA Publishing (a trading name of Automobile Association Developments Limited, whose registered office is Southwood East, Apollo Rise, Farnborough, Hampshire, GU14 0JW; registered number 1878835).

ISBN-10: 0-7495-4241-1
ISBN-13: 978-0-7495-4241-2

A01958

A CIP catalogue record for this book is available from the British Library.

Printed and bound in China

COLORS OF

Paris

CONT

ENTS

COLORS OF **PARIS**

COLORS OF PARIS: **INTRODUCTION**

P aris is the most beautiful city in the world. Some might argue for Venice, but no other city anywhere is a contender to the title. Lovers of Paris would say that this is a fact, not a point of view.

The beauty of Paris is a feeling as well as a fact. Its bistros give the impression that this is where candlelit dining was invented—indeed, it might be where romance itself was invented, and still thrives. It is a city for lovers, for honeymooners, for those celebrating anniversaries, and those remembering old times. It is a city to fall in love in for the first time in your life.

It is a city you also fall in love with. And love for Paris is as hard to define as love itself. It's in the flow of the river, the curve of the bridges that cross it, and the buildings you see either side, from the Eiffel Tower past the Musée d'Orsay and the former royal palace at the Louvre and on past Notre-Dame. It's the way in which modern design, such as the glass pyramid entrance to the Louvre or the in-your-face primary colors of the Pompidou Center, somehow blend in with the classical, the art nouveau, and the medieval buildings that make up this city's public face.

Its public face is also the graceful curves and sharp angles of the tree-lined boulevards, the city carved out in the late 19th century by town-planner Baron Georges-Eugène Haussmann. The legacy of Haussmann endures, enhanced by his heirs who, for the most part, have built on his design and kept the city a cohesive entity.

Meet the Neighborhoods

It has become a cliché to describe the cities of the world as being no more than collections of small villages, but in many ways you could describe Paris as one large village. Every quarter of the city has its local bars, its bakery, its cafés, its butcher, its street market: all those things you can find in almost every village throughout France. They give a reassuring familiarity when exploring unfamiliar areas, which is something every visitor should do, to savor the full flavor of Paris.

To get your bearings, remember that central Paris is divided into districts called *arondissements*, from one through twenty, which radiate out in a clockwise manner. The 1st, the 5th, and the 6th districts are on the Left Bank, Montmartre is in the 18th arondissement, and so on.

In a short visit most people will naturally head for the main attractions, flocking here and there, packing everything in; but for those who have more time, Paris is such a rewarding place to wander in, especially if you can get to know a neighborhood. Drop into the local bar, café, or shop more than once, and chances are you'll start to be greeted like a regular. And remember, *toujours la politesse*: always politeness. Even in Paris, most people say a cheery *bonjour* to greet each other before embarking on a conversation, or simply ordering a cup of coffee.

That's not to say that the neighborhoods aren't different, of course. If you want to see a fashion-conscious Parisian lady strutting her stuff, poodle, or man in tow, then you're more likely to see her in the Faubourg St-Honoré, while the jazz and bohemian set have always favored the Latin Quarter on the Left Bank, just along from the intellectual élite around the Sorbonne. The Marais, traditionally the Jewish area of Paris, is now both the Jewish and the gay area. Pigalle is the red light district, next to the artists' quarter of Montmartre.

The Main Attractions

The city's big pulling-points are spread around several districts, so even the short-term visitor will see quite a bit of the city—especially its métro system—while taking in the sights. The big draw is always the Eiffel Tower, and no matter how many times you've glimpsed it in movies or photos, seeing it in its wrought-iron reality, all 18,000 bits of it, can't fail to excite.

The same goes for the city's other major landmarks, such as the Arc de Triomphe, with no fewer than 12 streets radiating from it, at the center of place Charles de Gaulle, also known as l'Etoile, or the Star. Look west from here and on a clear day you can just see the modern arch at La Défense, while in the opposite direction a third arch stands, outside the Louvre.

The Louvre, the Musée d'Orsay, and the city's other major galleries and museums help to explain why Paris attracts visitors, in many cases again and again. In some ways the city has too much fine art for its own good, something you might think while trying to catch a glimpse of the *Mona Lisa*, the *Venus de Milo* or the works of Vincent van Gogh over the heads of tour groups. But there are other pulls, not always quite so packed, such as the Picasso Museum and the Rodin Museum, either of which is worth a few hours of your time, while the Louvre demands a few days, and the Musée d'Orsay has to be seen for the building (it used to be a railroad station) as much as what's inside it.

Even older buildings must be sought out too, or perhaps first simply prioritized, as there are so many of them to take in: the cathedral of Notre-Dame, the churches of Sacré-Coeur and Sainte-Chapelle, and grand edifices such as the Panthéon (burial place of Paris's greatest citizens), and Les Invalides, which contains the tomb of one of the greatest of them all, Napoleon Bonaparte. These are perhaps the greatest sights in Paris, although the best memories are usually the minor delights, the personal discoveries in this city of fashion, food, art, and architecture—the little local church, the bag bought in a market, the painting discovered in a junk shop, and the neighborhood bistro where you have the kind of meal you'll be dining out on for years.

Architect I. M. Pei placed this stunning glass pyramid in the cours Napoleon to great effect. When the plans were unveiled they caused much controversy, but the structure, surrounded by fountains and contrasting with the original building, is truly memorable. The entrance to the museum is through the pyramid.

The Cook's Tour

One of the enduring myths about Paris is that you have to pay a fortune to eat well there. Any regular visitor will dismiss that as nonsense. What is true is that if you want to eat some of the best food in the world, from the kitchens of top chefs such as Alain Ducasse and Guy Savoy, then you will pay for the privilege. To eat from a menu devised by Alain Ducasse is one of the best dining experiences anyone will ever have, for most people a once-in-a-lifetime event, never to be forgotten.

However, you can eat well at hundreds of restaurants throughout the city, at much lower prices than you would pay for the same standard of food elsewhere in the world. Good food is a given in Paris. It is part of the culture. The average diner in Paris knows a great deal about food and wine, and is not afraid to let the waiter know if a dish or a drink disappoints. Any eating place will forget that at their peril. That's not to say that you will never have a bad meal there, but if you go armed with a reputable good food guide then you could happily eat out every night for a year.

You needn't limit yourself to classical French cooking either. Some of the best food is the hearty fare provided by regional restaurants, where chefs from the Auvergne, Provence, Normandy, or Lyon will provide platefuls of their local specialties. France's colonial past means that there are numerous

North African restaurants too, so if you are eating on a budget, there is still plenty of choice, from Normandy crêpes to Tunisian couscous.

Impressions of Paris

It's not only in the kitchen that there have been cross-cultural exchanges with North Africa. French artists were frequent travelers to Tunisia, for example, where the dazzling colors and bright African light impacted on their work. And Paris has impacted on the work of every one of the countless artists who have lived in the city, over the centuries. The names are well-known, of course—Vincent Van Gogh, Pablo Picasso, Henri de Toulouse-Lautrec, Paul Gaugin, Claude Monet, Edouard Manet, Auguste Rodin. Can any other city boast such a roll-call?

Then there are the lesser-known artists too, some of whom might have an equally profound impact on the visitors of today, whether artists themselves or just travelers, if they take the trouble to seek their works out: Aristide Maillol, for example, whose sculptures grace the Jardin des Tuileries, yet whose museum on the rue de Grenelle is missed by most visitors; as is the museum in Pigalle devoted to the symbolist painter Gustave Moreau.

It's the Impressionists and those that they influenced who are the superstars of Paris art, though, and the Musée d'Orsay has one of the best collections in the world, including Manet's celebrated *Le Déjeuner sur l'Herbe* (1863). And to stand and see the great daubs of color that Van Gogh applied to the canvas, to be close enough to feel the passion he invested them with—that close connection with the past, and with tormented genius, is one of the powerful rewards of a visit to Paris.

Eighteen statues by Aristide Maillol were donated to the Jardin des Tuileries in the 1960s by Dina Vierny. Maillol used Vierny as his model after they met when she was very young. The statue above right, is entitled *Air*.
Next pages: Painting the art in the Musée d'Orsay.

A CONVENTION NATIONALE

Paris in Words

A picture may be worth a thousand words, but there have been thousands of words written about Paris by authors of all nationalities over the centuries. They paint a portrait every bit as vivid as a painting or photograph. Two of its finest writers, Victor Hugo and Honoré de Balzac, have small museums devoted to them. Emile Zola, creator of the 20 linked titles that became known as the Rougon-Macquart series, and arguably the greatest writer of them all, is honored with a tomb in the Panthéon, alongside illustrious figures such as Voltaire, Louis Braille and Victor Hugo. Others may lack a permanent shrine but their words live on in the city, as the city lives on in their words. Marcel

Proust, author of the multi-volume *A la Recherche du Temps Perdu* (Remembrance of Things Past, begun in 1912 and still unfinished at his death in 1922), is probably the best of these.

Another author not noted for his brevity was the Irishman James Joyce, a regular visitor and occasional resident. His book *Ulysses* (1922), regarded by many scholars and readers as the greatest novel of the 20th century, was first published in Paris when no other country in the world would touch it. The publisher was Shakespeare and Company, primarily a bookshop, which still exists down by the Seine. Fellow Irishman Samuel Beckett, author of *Waiting for Godot* (1953), lived in Paris for most of his life and is now a permanent resident in the cemetery at Montparnasse. And Oscar Wilde is buried at Père Lachaise, having died in a lackluster Paris hotel room where, on his death bed, he allegedly produced his last-known witticism: 'Either that wallpaper goes, or I do.'

In some ways, one of the best portraits of Paris was produced by another foreign writer and temporary resident of the city, the American Nobel Prize winner, Ernest Hemingway. His memoir of his time in Paris in the 1920s, *A Moveable Feast*, published in 1964 three years after his death, is a marvelous evocation of a time and a place, a Paris of bohemian writers and artists, living the good life though often in poverty, a time whose spirit lives on and haunts the Left Bank still today.

Paris in the Movies

It was in the shadows of Notre-Dame that many people's first impressions of Paris might have been gained, from seeing Charles Laughton starring in *The Hunchback of Notre-Dame*. From that 1939 classic through movies as diverse as *Les Enfants du Paradis* (1945), *Last Tango in Paris* (1972), Woody Allen's *Everyone Says I Love You* (1996), also shot around Notre-Dame, and more recently the

The Eiffel Tower (left) rises above neon-lit streets. Detail of the facade of the Folies Bergère (above left). Among the greats buried in the Pantheon (above) are writers Victor Hugo, Voltaire and Emile Zola. Père-Lachaise cemetery (right) is the resting place of authors, artists and musicians.

delightful *Amélie* (2002), Paris has been the setting for countless films. They all help create an image of the city in our minds, even if image and reality are often miles apart.

It is fitting that Paris should feature so strongly, as it was here that cinema—both the word and the industry—was created. The Lumière brothers invented their *cinématographe* machine, from which we get the word 'cinema,' in 1895, and were soon treating crowds to such masterpieces as a train arriving in a station, and a woman feeding her baby.

It's no surprise that we see Paris as a city of romance, intrigue, beauty, laughter, and matters risqué when you consider the early films that were made there, before modern reality took hold (yes, they named *cinéma verité* too. And avant garde.) In 1951 Gene Kelly was *An American in Paris*; in 1954 Jean Renoir (son of the artist Pierre-Auguste) made *French Can-Can*; in 1958 Louis Malle made *Les Amants* (The Lovers) with Jeanne Moreau; in 1960, Jean-Paul Belmondo's petty gangster effortlessly seduced another American in Paris, Jean Seberg, in Jean-Luc Godard's *A Bout de Souffle* (Breathless); in 1963 Cary Grant and Audrey Hepburn were falling in love in *Charade*; and in 1968 François Truffaut made Paris as much of a star as his actors in *Baisers Volés* (Stolen Kisses), the third of his series of semi-autobiographical films made entirely in the city.

The Nuts and Bolts of It

It's the way that Paris invents and re-invents itself that is one of its charms. The breathtaking revamp of the Musée d'Orsay is just one example, where an old railroad station became a bright and airy museum. The interior was transformed into a space that raises the spirits, and much of the old building's appeal was retained, including the station clock.

So many cities junk the old in favor of the new, and a new look which turns out to be old hat after a few years. Paris often preserves the old, though not always. The centuries-old wholesale food market at Les Halles was ripped out from the heart of the city, partly for practical reasons as the city's streets were no place for vast trucks fetching produce in and out. The shopping development that replaced it is one of the city's few eyesores—although it does have great shopping.

Other transformations have been much more successful. The most exciting part of the Musée Nationale de l'Histoire Naturelle (National Natural History Museum), the Evolution Gallery, is housed in a steel-and-glass structure built in 1889 and refurbished in the 1990s with the help of theater designer René Allio. The theatrical touch certainly shows, and it is well worth getting away from the honeypot sites, as essential as they are, to discover places like this.

And the more you discover places like this, and the mansions in the Marais, the secret parks, the hidden canals, even unexpected underground treasures like the sewers and the catacombs, the more you'll realize that there is no other contender. Paris is the most beautiful city in the world.

Paris's catacombs hold the remains of millions of former citizens. The walls above are formed by the skulls and bones of its residents. The catacombs were Paris's answer to overflowing cemeteries. Miles of tunnels were excavated and bones moved from cemeteries to this final resting place.

The Musée d'Orsay is in the building of a former railroad station and hotel on the banks of the Seine. Dominating the main hall is the original ornate station clock. In 1986 the museum opened, its works covering the years 1848 to 1914 and including an important Impressionist collection.

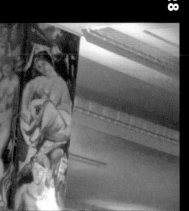

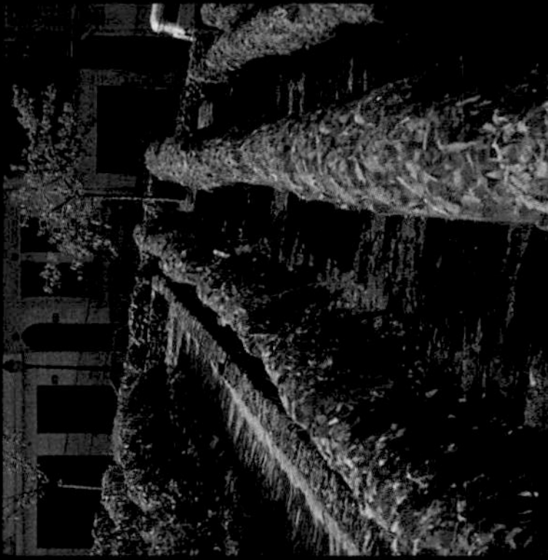

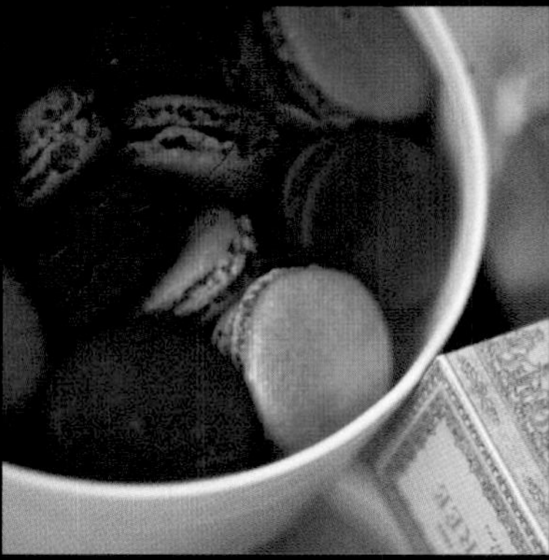

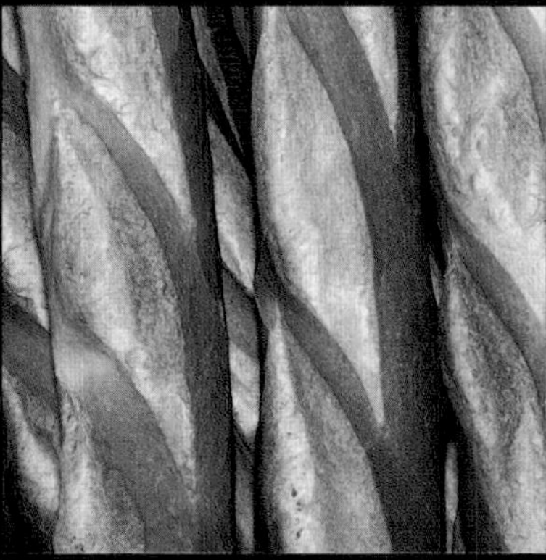

PARISIAN PALETTE

The whole of Paris is one large kitchen. It is, quite literally, a feast for the eyes, the nose, and ultimately the taste buds. If there is one passion that defines Parisians more than any other, more than fashion, more than art, more than politics, it is their love of food. And not only at meal times. Pedestrians can sample menus all day long simply by looking in shop windows, from the most humble corner grocery, where goods will nevertheless be displayed with flair, to the luxurious gourmet food store.

From simple treats such as bread, cheese, and coffee, through to the delights of fresh fish, rich chocolate, and of course, fine wine, Parisians appreciate the best things in life, and present them with an artist's eye—truly a palette for the palate.

It may be a market stand simply selling tomatoes, onions, cheeses, and snails, or a specialist store such as Fauchon (above left and right), but food in Paris is always arranged to be irresistible. Parisians are said to be notoriously chauvinistic, and this is certainly true as far as French wine is concerned.

Only wine made in the Champagne region (about an hour east of Paris) can be called champagne, so there is no need even to check the labels on the bottles cooling at La Coupole (above center). But everywhere you will find the finest ingredients from around the world: rum from Guadeloupe,

vanilla pods from Madagascar, and the best Iranian caviar. Food that looks too good to eat. Almost.

CAFÉ CULTURE

To the Parisian, the café is far more than the pub is to the Englishman, or the bar to the New Yorker. The Americans discovered Starbucks but Parisians have been meeting in cafés for the last few hundred years. And it is unthinkable that a café could serve only coffee, and not wine.

What could be more civilized than to sit outside in the sun with a *pichet* (one-person carafe) of *vin du pays* and catch up on the day's news, which may include the startling information that the first Starbucks has arrived in the French capital. *Quelle horreur!*

The waiter (above left) in his traditional uniform of black trousers, white shirt, and natty black vest, is a familiar figure in Paris, and a respected one. To be a waiter is no stop-gap job, it is a career in itself and as esteemed as any other occupation.

Boundaries blur in Paris. Is it a bar, a café, a bistro, or a brasserie? In many cases, it scarcely matters. Bars and cafés are for drinking, though some serve snacks or even have full meal menus.

Around any of the city's great railroad stations, bars and cafés abound, like this bistro at Montparnasse (above center). What better way to wait for the train bringing your lover than with a coffee or a glass of wine?

The bistro and the classic brasserie are for eating, though in many you can enjoy just a drink if you wish. The original brasseries, of which many still survive, served only beer ('brasserie' means brewery). Now some are among Paris's best dining experiences.

PIERRE LESCOT
SALON
AU PERE
TRANQUILLE
SALLE AU PREMIER
VUE SUR FORUM

From the former market district of Les Halles (left) to the haunts of the literati like the Café de Flore (above) on the Left Bank, Paris has a café for everyone, and everyone has his or her café.

ELEVATED
DINING

Who could imagine Paris without the Eiffel Tower? Many would like to. The writer Guy de Maupassant said that he liked to dine at the Tower, as then he didn't have to look at it. Diners today pay highly for the privilege of a view. Diners in the highest restaurant in Europe, the Ciel de Paris (left) in the Montparnasse Tower, can gaze toward diners in the two restaurants in the Eiffel Tower itself, no doubt themselves gazing back toward Montparnasse.

La Coupole in Montparnasse is the epitome of art deco dining, where Pablo Picasso, Ernest Hemingway, and many others have emptied their plates and filled—and refilled—their glasses since it was opened in 1927.

The nation that invented the notion of eating chocolate for breakfast obviously has a serious love affair with what the rest of the world regards as an indulgence. And the *pain au chocolat* or chocolate croissant is only the beginning...

In Paris the good *chocolatier* is as highly regarded as the best Michelin-rated chef. Names such as Jean-Paul Hévin are lauded with awards. London's stylish Savoy Hotel even buys its chocolate from Hévin's chocolate shop (above), near the Jardin du Luxembourg.

JEAN-PAUL HÉVIN
CHOCOLATIER
— PARIS —

Chocolate has its own fan club in Paris. Known as the *Club des Croqueurs de Chocolat*, its members meet regularly to discuss the latest creations from the city's ever-inventive *chocolatiers*, some of whom travel the world to discover new flavors, new combinations, and the best new chocolate.

Chocolate arrived in Paris in the 17th century, and the city's first chocolate shop was opened in 1659 in the rue de l'Arbre Sec in the fashionable Faubourg St-Honoré, whose shops (above right) still serve up the most desirable luxury treats today.

PARIS VINEYARD

The French say that a day without wine is like a day without love, but there is no danger of that happening in Paris. The love affair with the grape is as strong now as it ever was—provided it is a French grape. Few foreign wines meet with the Parisian's approval.

Once a prime wine-growing region that rivaled Bordeaux, today Montmartre can boast only about 2,000 vines (above left). *Tant pis*, as the French say: never mind. It is enough to produce 1,000 bottles of Clos Montmartre (above right) every October.

Montmartre's vines are a mix of varieties, including gamay and pinot noir. The resulting blend is bottled and auctioned for charity on the first Sunday in October (right). Most is immediately unbottled again and drunk, exhibiting that familiar Parisian *joie de vivre*.

PLACES & FACES

Paris has a thousand faces and all of us have our favorites. For some it is the fine food and wine, for others fashion, or architecture, and for many, of course, it is the city of romance. Romance can be found under the bridges of Paris, down by the Seine with me (in the words of the song), or in the sidewalk cafés. It may begin after dark when the brasserie lights come on and the cobbled streets are bathed in rainbows. Even in the rain, Paris can look good.

In the rain or in the sun, Paris is a city for people. It is a city where you might see a unicyclist weaving along the sidewalk, or rollerbladers slicing through the traffic. It is a city that builds a beach for itself in the summer, where children play, and old folk watch them, and all ages in between seem permanently in love.

On the Champs-Elysées at night (above), even a pizza parlor can look romantic. Here people need nothing more than good companions, a tasty meal, a glass of wine, and the sheer joy of being in the world's most beautiful city.

Once there were fields here, then a royal gardener planted trees along what became the Champs-Elysées, the Elysian Fields. To the ancient Greeks, they were a paradise, where people pursued their favorite pleasures, and worries were left behind. They could have been describing Paris.

The scene above is Montmartre but it could be any of a number of districts—the Marais, Bastille, St-Germain—where locals and visitors mingle and check out restaurant menus, looking for that special dish that tempts them inside.

Or, take away the cars and the fashions, and the scene could have been painted a hundred years ago, and more, by any of the artists who chose to make Montmartre their home for at least a part of their life.

PARISIANS

'I love Paris in the Springtime,' 'April in Paris,' 'I love Paris in the Fall,' 'How would you like to be, down by the Seine with me?' 'I was a Free Man in Paris,' 'An American in Paris,' 'The Last Time I saw Paris.'

Paris inspires not only artists, but songwriters too, who try to capture its mood and its magic not in images but in words. An even harder task; almost as hard as trying to pin down the meaning of love.

Paris is known as the City of Light but it should be renamed the City of Love, for no other city on earth makes a better backdrop for the glances and kisses of lovers, the hand-holding of sweethearts young and old.

Love makes the world go round, and certainly makes the world of advertising go round, in Paris as much as anywhere else. Huge billboards in the métro or on the street (above), are often provocative. As another song has it: 'Anything Goes.'

But lovers only have eyes for each other, sealing their love with a stolen kiss, a touch, a glance, or a quiet moment together like this couple (opposite, top left) on the bank of the Seine, simply watching the river flow.

For others, that intimate moment overwhelms even the most stunning locations—the enchanting Île de la Cité (opposite, top right), the Parisians' favorite park, the Jardin du Luxembourg (bottom right), or what many feel is the loveliest square in the city, the place des Vosges (bottom left).

THE DAY BEGINS

A cup of coffee, a crablike croissant, a moment of calm. In the Latin Quarter (left) tables are being laid ready for *petit déjeuner* (breakfast) and the chairs wait in rows, like a theater auditorium anticipating its audience.

CHILDREN

The Church of the Sacred Heart, Sacré-Coeur (above), watches over Paris from the city's highest point. To the casual visitor, it is a photo opportunity, one of the top sights to see. To the children it is no more than a familiar backdrop to their games.

When you know that the church was built as a memorial to the 58,000 French soldiers who were killed in the Franco-Prussian War of 1870–71, the sight of the playing children becomes a poignant reminder of how a city and a nation rebuilds itself.

Rebuilds but also remembers, as the church remains open all day and all night, its priests praying constantly for the souls of the dead. On the terrace outside, visitors look outward at one of the most memorable views in the city.

For the children of Paris, the streets are both playground and classroom. So too, on occasion, are the city's museums, as anyone who has ever shared an exhibition room with a noisy school group will know.

Outside the church of St-Eustache (above left), visitors usually find the sculpture *L'Ecoute* (Listening) by Henri de Miller quite arresting. For this youngster, it is more a case of simply resting.

The group (above right), however, have obviously been gripped, their innocent young faces attentive to whatever their teacher is telling them. Or perhaps they are watching a puppet show, a magician, a fire-eater, or one of the city's many other street entertainers.

STREET FARE

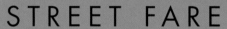

Fast food with a French flair is one of the eating options open to both locals and visitors who are in a hurry. This street vendor in Montmartre (above) enjoys making the fresh *crêpe* just as much as his customer will enjoy eating it.

There are few streets in Paris where it is possible to walk more than a few yards without coming across some temptation or other, most frequently involving food and drink, and this street in Montparnasse (top right) is obviously no exception.

Other street temptations include the city's many markets, and even those aimed squarely at visitors, like this one in Montmartre (bottom right) will have something—such as these piles of brightly colored T-shirts—that loudly shouts 'Paris.'

DECORATIVE SPLENDOR

Shopping and eating can be simple or accompanied by great Parisian style. The 1823 Galerie Vivienne (top) near the Palais Royal has ornate cast-iron gates behind which are stores ranging from a bookshop dating back to 1826 to Jean-Paul Gaultier's exclusive fashion temple.

At the Gare du Nord, train passengers come and go, few knowing of the fabulous 1880s decor in the nearby restaurant, Julien, where this lady (left) with her Pre-Raphaelite looks gazes down on the diners tucking in to foie gras and pigs' trotters.

Le Train Bleu restaurant (above) in the Gare de Lyon, with its Belle-Epoque interior, harks back to an age when traveling by train was an experience, not an endurance—as was the food to be had at these mainline stations.

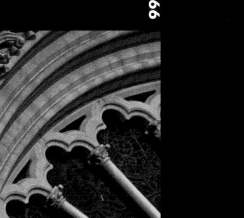

MODERNIST

For the most part, the Paris skyline has altered little over the last few centuries, and skyscrapers have been left to New York. Look, the Parisians say: tall buildings can be beautiful in isolation. One of the few, the Montparnasse Tower (above left), built in 1973, soars 59 stories into the sky.

Some of the boldest modern experiments have taken place in the suburbs, regenerating them and bringing workers and visitors alike to places such as the futuristic Parc de la Villette, where this spectacular steel sphere (above center) houses the Géode cinema.

The Grande Arche de La Défense (right), designed by Danish architect Otto von Spreckelsen, is some 3 miles (5km) west of the Arc de Triomphe but in a direct line with Napoleon's structure and with the arch outside the Louvre, whose glass roof (far right) also blends ancient and modern.

History will be the judge. Modern architects constantly have to remind themselves of that whenever they are designing a new building for Paris. Nothing escapes the merciless gaze of the Parisians, and few buildings that make up the cityscape today have avoided a tongue-lashing from contemporary critics. The Eiffel Tower? Tear it down. Sacré-Coeur and the Arc de Triomphe? Monstrosities. The Louvre's pyramid, the Pompidou Center, the Montparnasse Tower? Stains on the face of the city. But history has been the judge, and welcomed them.

POMPIDOU CENTER

To create an art gallery that is itself a work of art was another controversial triumph for the planners of Paris. An Englishman (Richard Rogers) and an Italian (Renzo Piano) designed it—a truly European venture.

Open walkways (above) and open spaces (right), an open piazza outside where street artists perform and people can relax, an eye-catching exterior with pipes in primary colors (following pages), a cinema, a restaurant, a talking point, a must-see. This is the Pompidou Center.

EIFFEL TOWER

What can be said that has not yet been said? What can be seen that has not yet been shown? The Eiffel Tower *is* Paris. And like the city of which it is a symbol, it does not disappoint.

Architect Gustave Eiffel had his own office in the tower for a time, and worked there until he died in 1923, some 34 years after the tower was, according to him, not designed but 'formed by the wind itself.'

So solid is this tower formed by the wind that even in the strongest gales it never sways more than 4 or 5 inches (10 or 12cm), despite weighing over 10,000 tons. In the heat of summer the iron girders expand by up to 6 inches (15cm).

No facts or statistics can ever convey the grandeur and sheer audacity that is the Eiffel Tower. To view it from afar when it is lit up at night is to share in a little of the magic that mankind can sometimes create.

NOTRE-DAME

Imagine a time when Paris was no more than a small town, where most buildings were tiny and temporary. Imagine approaching from north, south, east, or west, with a view that extended for miles over fields and low rooftops. Imagine, then, seeing Notre-Dame.

Imagine, too, the magnificent cathedral falling into decay and disrepair. This was its state in 1831 when Victor Hugo wrote *The Hunchback of Notre-Dame* (published in French as *Notre-Dame de Paris*). Hugo determined to save the building.

By 1841 enough money had been raised to start work on the restoration, which was to take 23 years but result in the building we see today, still standing proud on the Île de la Cité, where the city of Paris itself was born some 2,300 years ago.

Ignore the other visitors, and think instead of the people of the past who have walked under the Rose Window (above) and into Notre-Dame: Joan of Arc, who was tried here; Napoleon, who was crowned emperor here; King Charles I of England, who was married here. Think of these—and a hunchback scuttling up on the roof.

Power and peace. Notre-Dame (above) loses none of its sanctity, despite its 10 million annual visitors. To experience it best, attend a service, or the Sunday afternoon organ recital, when the music—and one's spirits—soar to the roof.

A Paris delight is the way that its grand sights—the Eiffel Tower, the Pompidou Center, or Sacré-Coeur (right)—appear unexpectedly at the turn of a corner, constantly giving new views of the city's architectural splendors, constantly seeming to re-invent themselves.

The former Orsay railroad station became the Musée d'Orsay (above), opening to the public in 1986 after nine years of conversion masterminded by Italian architect Gae Aulenti. The soaring glass-and-iron roof was designed by Victor Laloux for the station which opened in 1900. The original wildly ornate Belle-Epoque restaurant and ballroom are still intact. Overseeing the displays of sculptures in the main concourse is the former station clock. You will find stylish architectural flourishes at rail and métro stations around the city.

For all the grandeur of Paris, it is the city's street scenes which provide a constant feast for the visitor's eye. The plain shopfront or café, like this one in the Latin Quarter (above), delight with their simplicity. Paris is a city on a human scale.

Montmartre has always attracted artists; its buildings as well as its lifestyle appealed to them. Maurice Utrillo (1883–1955) painted this pastel pink restaurant (above), little-changed in the passing of a century of time.

VILLAGE PARIS

Vincent Van Gogh also lived in Montmartre for a time, and would have regularly passed this café (left) with its archetypal Parisian blue shutters down the road from his apartment on the rue Lepic.

LANDMARKS & VIEWS

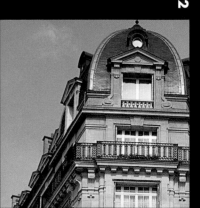

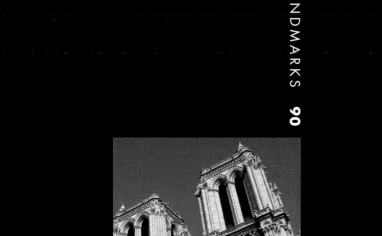

One visit to Paris is never enough. Visitors find themselves constantly drawn back to it, envying those who actually live there all year round, and see it in all its seasons, see its trees blossom and turn green, change to gold in the fall, then die to be reborn in spring.

The Paris you see before you is Haussmann's city. It is Napoleon's city, and the city of Proust. It is the city of Edith Piaf and of visiting writers like Ernest Hemingway. All add their own sparkle to this diamond.

Climb the Tower, and other towers. See the churches and cathedrals. Visit the galleries and read the books. Stroll in the boulevards and take a break in the sidewalk cafés. Even visit the famous cemeteries. Do all this, and soon Paris will be your city too.

VIEWPOINTS

Paris takes your breath away. What begins as a cliché—you go to Paris, you must go up the Eiffel Tower—becomes magical when it happens. As you rise, the city falls away below you, the horizon widens until, at the top, you feel you can see the curvature of the earth. From on high, you see how special Paris is. Streets as straight as arrows shoot off in all directions, and you realize how green the city is. You spot the landmarks—look, there's the Arc de Triomphe, and that must be Napoleon's tomb—and determine to visit those landmarks too; and you do, and look back toward the Tower, becoming more familiar with the City of Light every time you see it, and making it your own.

From the Montparnasse Tower (above) other views open, and a new neighborhood reveals itself to you. Its cemetery is where Samuel Beckett, Jean-Paul Sartre, and Simone de Beauvoir lie. Its train station conceals a hidden garden nearby, another Paris surprise.

From modernity to tradition (left): looking out from the Pompidou Center across a square to buildings from an earlier era.

Sitting at a pavement café (above) it's possible to appreciate the 'inside-out' design of Richard Rogers' and Renzo Piano's Pompidou Center.

HAUSSMANN

'Paris is the heart of France,' declared Napoleon III. 'Let's open new roads, make the populous neighborhoods which lack air and delight healthy, and may charitable light penetrate everywhere in our walls.' The man charged with changing Paris in the mid-19th century was Baron Georges-Eugène Haussmann. Over the course of 18 years, he tore down slums, built wide boulevards, designed parks, constructed railroad stations. His vision is everywhere, from Montparnasse (left), in the place des Victoires (top), and especially from the top of the Arc de Triomphe (above and right). While you gaze at the beauty of Haussmann's Paris, here laid out below the Arc de Triomphe, pause and consider another of his achievements. He also designed the sewer system. Below ground another Paris is laid out, each sewer labeled with the name of the street above it.

GREEN PARIS

If Paris is the heart of France, as Napoleon III declared, then his architect, Haussmann, knew that it also needed lungs, to breathe. Parisians today can still thank the Baron not only for the tree-lined streets, but also for the green spaces, large and small, that he created or preserved.

The Parc Monceau (left) pre-dates Haussmann and was created in 1778 by the Duc de Chartres. Although scarcely half a mile (1km) from the Arc de Triomphe, few visitors discover its hidden charms.

The Jardin des Tuileries (above) were once part of the old Tuileries Palace and the preserve of royalty. Today all enjoy their gardens and trees, their park benches, playground, and art galleries. The view past the place de la Concorde to the Arc de Triomphe also raises the spirits.

The Jardin du Luxembourg (top) sprawls over 60 acres (24 ha) and attractions range from a bandstand for concerts to a bee-keeping school. In the 1920s the starving author Ernest Hemingway admitted to catching pigeons here, to put in the pot.

Most Parisians live in apartments without gardens, which is why their parks are so important to them. They also bring their gardens indoors, buying blooms from the lovely flower market (above) on the Île de la Cité, near Notre-Dame.

Look on a map of Paris and the main parks are clearly visible, both the well-known, such as the Jardin du Luxembourg, or the quieter Parc Monceau (above). The city is also sandwiched between the huge Bois de Boulogne to the west and the Bois de Vincennes, to the east.

However, it is the secret green spaces the visitor needs to uncover, and Paris is good at concealing its greatest treasures, making you seek them out, or perhaps allowing you to discover them by accident.

On the traffic-filled place de la Bastille, few would think that a delightful park is nearby, built over a disused overhead railroad line that ran along the avenue Daumesnil. Those who search behind Gare Montparnasse for the concealed Jardin Atlantique, above the railroad tunnel are well rewarded.

LANDMARKS

NAPOLEON

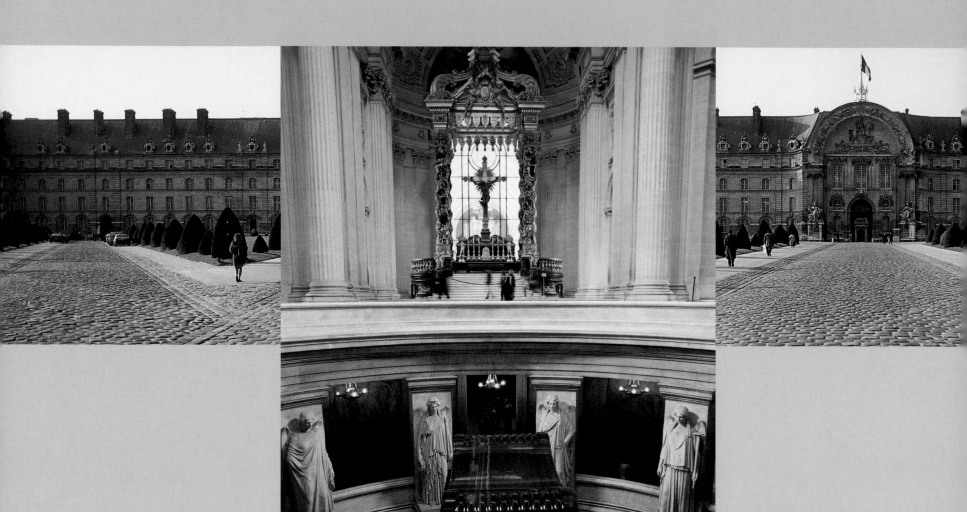

From many places in Paris, a golden dome on the left bank of the river can be seen. To the new visitor it attracts curiosity. It is a grand and glistening eye-catcher; but is it a cathedral, a church, or a public building?

It is, in fact, La Dôme, or to give it its full title, the Eglise du Dôme, the church of the Dôme. But it is what lies beneath the dome that matters, and you should let it draw you toward it.

For directly beneath the Dôme's spire, in a vast circular vault below the ground, lies the tomb of perhaps the greatest Frenchman who ever lived: Napoleon Bonaparte. From humble beginnings he became the Emperor of France, and for a time the conqueror of much of Europe.

About a dozen old soldiers still live in the Hôtel des Invalides, behind which Napoleon's tomb stands. When it was built in the late 17th century, over 6,000 wounded soldiers moved in. Today it is a monument to the greatest French soldier of them all.

CULTUR
& STYLE

méi

For the fashion-conscious, a visit to Paris can be overwhelming. Names previously seen only in style magazines and on TV are there, on the store-fronts. Chanel, Dior, Nina Ricci, Ungaro, Prada, Calvin Klein, Laroche, Valentino, and Louis Vuitton—and that's only the avenue Montaigne.

But a shopping trip intermingles with other aspects of French culture. Authors Sinclair Lewis and Henry James both lived on this elegant street, and the first chef to win six Michelin stars, Alain Ducasse, has his restaurant there in the Hôtel Plaza Athénée.

There are bargains too, such as these simple but stylish and fun shopping bags, brightening up a street market (above). The market in the place d'Aligre is also good for shabby-chic fabrics, popular with young designers, who can often be found rummaging among the colorful cloths.

rue Royale - 75008 Paris - Tel.: 01 40 17 07 40
Bonaparte - 75006 Paris - Tel.: 01 56 24 15 60
www.swarovski.com

794 PDB 75

SHOPPING

Fashion, food, style, art, music, literature—even the popular culture of soccer, where France became the world champions in 2000—at all these things and more, the French excel. And in Paris they come together and blend into one glorious mix. It's street art, it's cutting-edge fashion. It's the exclusive fashion stores on the avenue Montaigne, and it's the grungy street markets where the fashion designers themselves go to find material and inspiration. It's the artists painting tourist portraits in Montmartre, and it's the memories of artists past that linger in the air there. It's Paris.

You might think that everything in Paris is outrageously expensive. Not so, though some visitors choose to buy something small by a big name, as a fashion accessory. Whether they feel quite like the model on the opposite page (above left) is another matter. You might remember those shops specializing shops (though in Paris it's another of the city's charms that you can expect to stumble upon shops selling only mustard, or stationery, hats or dresses, selling only umbrellas, or cookbooks).

Colors, fabrics, shapes, a stylish walk, a glance. You can buy the clothes, but you cannot buy the cool, the sophistication, the slightly haughty knowing look that tells of a lifetime of living, and flirting, in Paris.

Paris was among the first cities to come up with the idea of personal shoppers. In some shops and department stores, assistants listen to your needs and explore the shelves to bring you what they think you are looking for—or perhaps what they think you might need.

Temptation is everywhere, from the green sunglasses in the chic rue du Faubourg St-Honoré (far top left) to the cutting-edge provocation of Jean-Paul Gaultier (above left).

ABSTRACT

Nothing is simple in Paris; not even the simple things. The simplest food can often be the most sophisticated. A métro station can be a work of art. So too can a shop window display. Children's clothes can be haute couture.

Outside the multipurpose Pompidou Center is a fountain (above). This too is a work of art, inspired by Igor Stravinsky's Firebird Suite. It's also a piece of entertainment for children—and adults—firing water at those who pause to look.

And these objects (right)? A modern art installation, perhaps, or a children's adventure playground? Neither. They are stools from the Dom Christian Koban shop in the Marais, where kooky kitchenware lines up alongside household items you never knew you needed.

Art isn't just in museums in Paris, but outside them too, like the famous statue *The Thinker* (left), whose naked frame is exposed to the elements in the gardens of the Musée-Rodin.

The Puget statues (top) contemplate their life outside the Louvre, while even bridges, such as the Pont Alexandre III (above) cause passersby to pause and admire these examples from the Belle-Epoque period.

STREET LIFE

Art is not merely high art. Life is art in Paris, and art is life. On the streets there are classical guitarists, like the man above, and musician-artists, like this Montmartre woman whose traditional French accordion is linked to her fun umbrella.

Even mime artists have style in Paris. Forget those figures painted all-white or all-gold, seen in every city in the world. Here in Paris is a businessman-mime in Montmartre, and (right) an explorer-mime in the place de la Sorbonne, the intellectual university quarter.

As long as you don't expect to have your portrait painted by the next Picasso, Toulouse-Lautrec, Gaugin, or van Gogh, all of whom worked in Montmartre, then getting an instant likeness is part of the fun of visiting the one-time village.

The place du Tertre is where the artists congregate, vying for custom in a low-key way, hoping the man will want a portrait of his wife, or the parents a painting of their young children. It's a cheap enough and unique souvenir.

Just as they did in the late 19th century, artists still need to make a living, they like the company of other artists, and, as with the lady above, they still like to work in cafés and bars. *Plus ça change*, the French say...

COMMERCIAL ART

Paris and posters have gone hand in hand since the form was invented in the 19th century. Artists such as Toulouse-Lautrec painted posters advertising cabaret shows, and depicting their dancers. The most famous of these was Jane Avril, and now *Jane Avril Dancing* is on display in the Musée d'Orsay.

Posters are everywhere, seen in restaurants and in museums. They are sold *en masse* in souvenir shops, but you might find some more unusual ones on the stalls of the old *bouquinistes* who sell books and comics, postcards, and posters from their wooden stalls alongside the Seine.

COLORS OF PARIS:
LIGHT & REFLECTIONS

ONS

THE EYES OF PARIS

In the 19th and 20th centuries, artists by the hundred settled in Paris, spending years trying to capture its many looks and forms. Every museum is packed with paintings of this enigmatic place. Photographers who have been captivated by the city include great names such as Henri Cartier-Bresson, Brassai, Man Ray, and Robert Doisneau. The 21st-century photographer can only give thanks for the invention of the digital camera, for only a camera that never runs out of film can hope to keep up with the endlessly changing faces and moods of Paris.

The streets of Montmartre (right) are where most artists settled, attracted like moths to a flame. It's an almost timeless scene, and possible to imagine a photographer in a hundred years returning to match this shot.

NIGHT LIGHT

Paris at night is a special experience, and the place to experience it is down by the Seine. Hours can pass, admiring the lights on the buildings, wandering this way and that, or pausing on the bridges, as travelers have done for centuries.

The iron-and-glass domes of the Grand Palais (above), built for the World Fair of 1900, are such a quintessential Parisian sight. The world may know it as the City of Light but Paris is equally seductive at night.

When the light goes out of the sky with the setting sun, the lights on the buildings start to glow and illuminate the city's other beauty. None is more beautiful than the Eiffel Tower, which glows above Paris like a beacon. The sight thrills every time, no matter how often repeated.

WATER'S EDGE

Paris life still revolves around the Seine, which snakes through the city like the living thing that it is. In some places, such as here on the Île St-Louis (left), you could almost be in a peaceful provincial town.

It's a feeling enhanced by the riverside trees, the pathways for strolling, and even the surprising sight of fishermen in the heart of the city. Paris never loses its human touch.

NEON

Paris may be romantic at night, but it is a reveler too, the sensitive woman who knows how to let her hair down. The innocent country windmill (opposite) becomes the Moulin Rouge, the Red Windmill, beckoning passersby to its cabaret.

Elsewhere, from Les Halles to the Marais to Harry's New York bar in the rue Daunou, neon rules. It was allegedly in Harry's that George Gershwin first had the idea to write *An American in Paris*. Its legendary cocktails still inspire today's Americans in Paris.

MIRRORS

Paris by day, Paris by night, Paris in neon: all faces of the City of Light. Paris reflects on itself too, and its contrasts are sometimes best appreciated in an unexpected reflection, when light and angle and design all come together at the same snatched moment.

In the ultramodern creations at La Défense (left), to the west of Paris, the innovative buildings fragment into a landscape that is almost from another planet, as if pulled apart and put back together by the viewer.

Modern sculptures in the courtyard of the ancient Palais Royal (above left), and graceful buildings reflected in a shop window (above right) both give their own little insights into what Paris is about.

When the old food market at Les Halles was torn down, Parisians were up in arms, but today they flock to the new buildings which replaced it (far left), and perhaps the old ones which surround it are appreciated all the more.

Visitors value the beautiful details; they are around us all the time in Paris but are occasionally pulled into focus by the photographer's keen eye, and we suddenly 'see' the shape of a lamp-post (top) or the curved grace of art nouveau stained glass.

TRANQUILITY

Previous pages: The place de la Concorde is usually seen as a racetrack traffic hub, a challenge to cross, and somewhere to be hurried from. But its floodlit fountains at night, with the Egyptian obelisk in the background, paint a very different picture.

In any city there are places to retreat to, to escape the crowds and traffic, and the woman above left can walk her poodle—what else?—in the Bois de Boulogne, over 2,000 acres (800 ha) of parkland, and parks within parks, west of the city center.

And in the heart of the city itself, the Medici Fountain and water feature in the Jardin du Luxembourg provides a restful break, a truly tranquil place to read, to chat, to gaze, or, quite simply, to be.

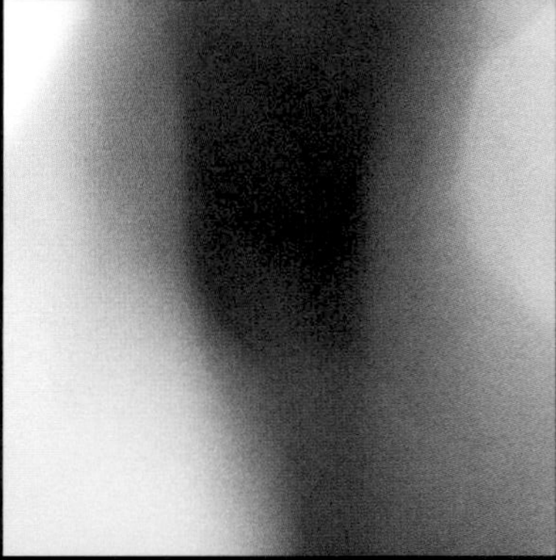

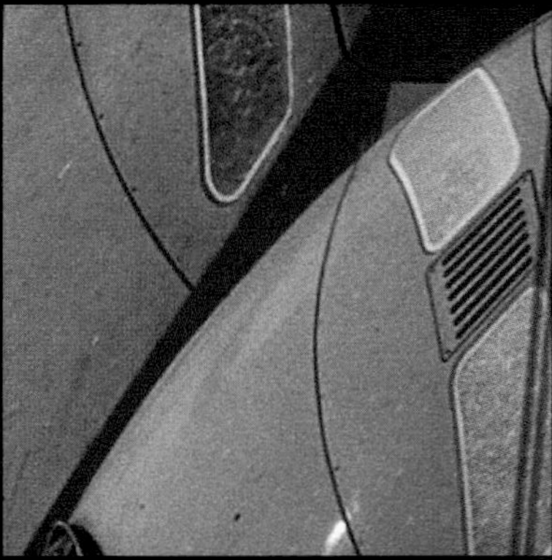

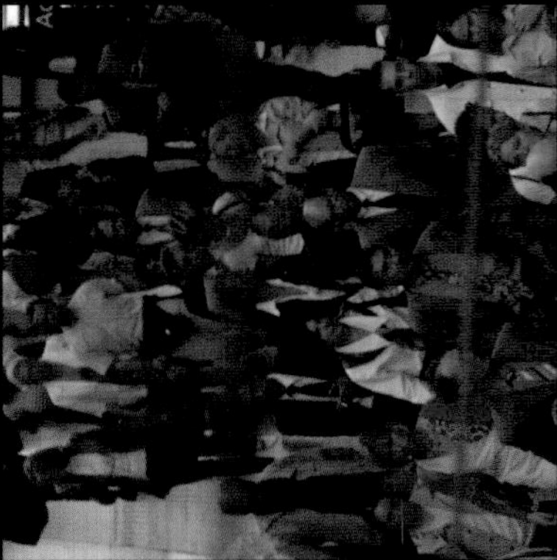

The Paris métro (top) has been transporting people across the city since 1900. You can travel quickly and easily from the ultramodern buildings at La Défense to the woods in the Bois de Boulogne and the château and lakes in the Bois de Vincennes.

A city with its peaceful places, but a city always on the move; people entering and leaving, going underground, people on the roads—always people on the roads, in cars, on buses, on bicycles. Even from time to time on rollerblades, a craze that Paris has really taken to its heart. Visitors mingle with commuters and locals, and though there are places where tourists travel to in their thousands, Paris never gives the impression of being a tourist trap. Its métro lets visitors move everywhere, easily, blending into the city's ever-changing, ever-moving panorama.

Since the opening of the Eurostar train link between Paris and London in 1994, both cities have seen an influx of visitors, for it is now quicker for Londoners to get to Paris, and Parisians to London, than it is for either to get to other parts of their own country.

At the Gare du Nord (above), visitors from the UK arrive and pour down the platform, passports at the ready, walking straight into the heart of Paris, less than three hours after leaving London.

GRAND VITESSE

Paris's train stations are impressive places, filled with the powerful lines of the TGV trains, *Trains à Grand Vitesse*, or more simply, high-speed trains. The TGVs link the city's six major stations with the rest of the country, and on into Europe.

It must be the language, but to the visitor, names such as Gare du Nord and Gare de l'Est have an exotic ring about them, suggesting great journeys to the regions of this diverse country.

In fact the names mean only the station for the north and for the east respectively. The Gare de Lyon (above) serves the south, and in August its platforms are packed with Parisians heading for their annual dose of summer sun.

ON THE ROAD

Even cops look chic in Paris, though they need more than smart looks to keep the city's traffic moving. In places like the Champs-Elysées (top right), driving requires another type of French flair altogether and pedestrians should take care.

Some people escape the traffic jams by zipping around on scooters and bicycles, and sometimes walking can be faster than some of the city's 15,000 taxi cabs. Parking is a challenge, but that too is often attempted with a certain style, and disregard for regulations.

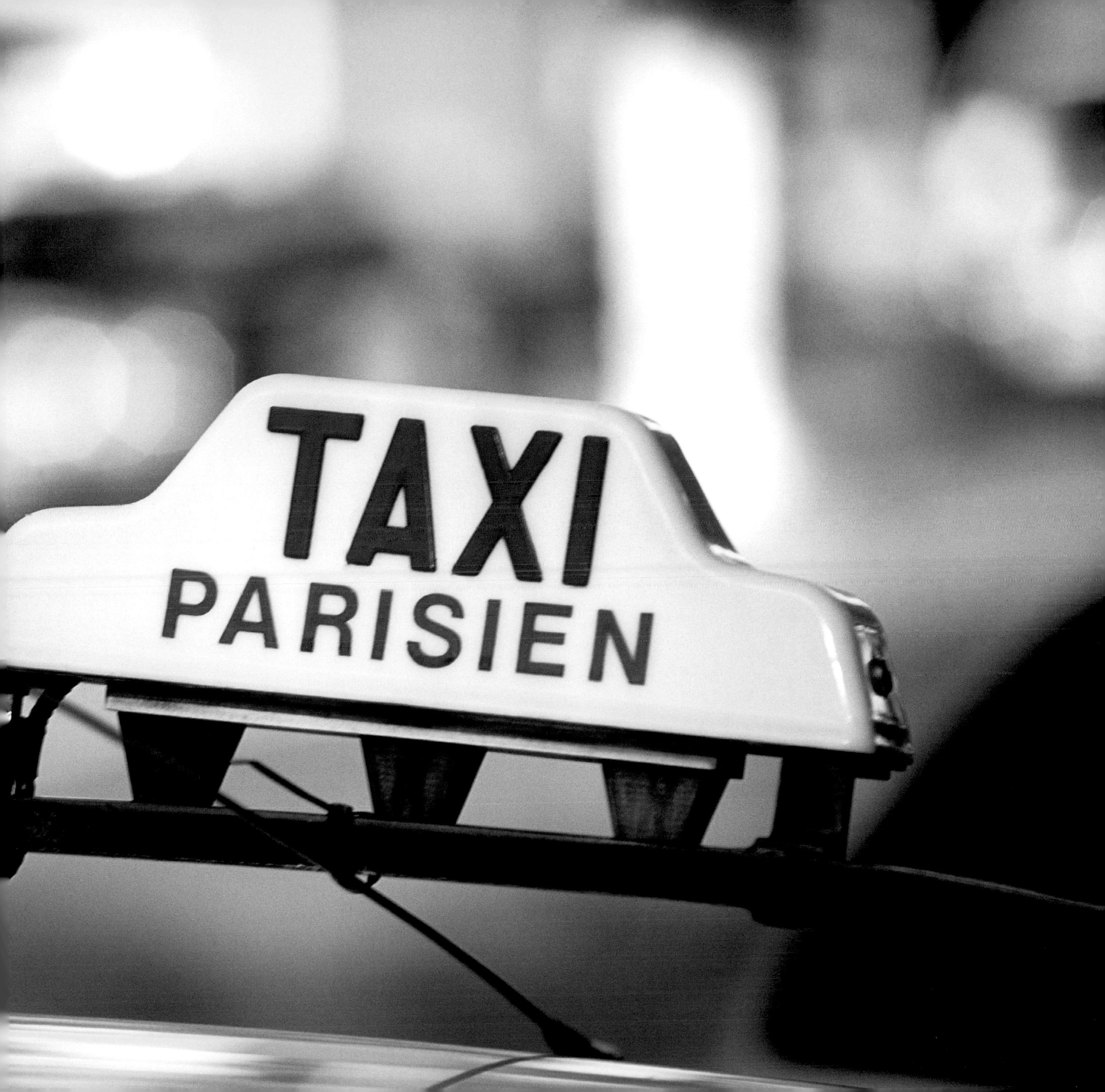
TAXI
PARISIEN

Paris à Vélo, or Paris by Bike, is just one of several bicycle rental and tour companies in the city. It may seem crazy, as you watch the traffic racing round the Bastille, but there are plenty of quieter back streets that are more vélo-friendly.

Rollerblading is more than a passing fad in Paris. The city's people have taken to it with great enthusiasm, as a way of getting around that is both practical and has a sense of style, of being different, which appeals to every Parisian's heart.

There are even special rollerblading tours, every Friday evening and Sunday afternoon, when eco-minded visitors join thousands of local families, like this one (above), to see the city, have fun, and keep fit, all at the same time. As many as 12,000 people have been known to turn up.

If you can't beat them, join them. This rollerblading cop (top right) keeps up with one of the special events, although normally rollerblades are not allowed to ride in the traffic, or on the sidewalks along the Champs-Elysées.

For those who prefer more traditional means of getting around, a stroll along the banks of the Seine by the *bouquinistes* is hard to beat. These second-hand booksellers have plied their trade in the shadow of Notre-Dame for centuries now.

BATEAU

Some visitors to cities scoff at the tours on offer, preferring not to do the same things as countless others. In Paris this would be a mistake, for boat tours especially give you a different take on the city and its riverfront architecture.

Glorious views of Notre-Dame (far left) can be had, by day or by night. Some evening river cruises, with dinner included, serve excellent food, and surely there is nothing more romantic than sitting at a candle-lit table while the loveliest city in the world glides right by.

SEASONS

'April in Paris, chestnuts in blossom...' so the old song goes, although every season is a good season, if you spend it in Paris, the city of food and of fashion, the city of art and artists, the city of love and romance.

In summer the Parisians themselves depart for the sun, leaving the city a quieter place. Though some restaurants may close, Paris itself opens up to offer more space, a less frenetic pace, blue skies, and sidewalks filled with strolling couples with smiles on their faces.

The Arc de Triomphe was built to commemorate Napoleon's victory at the Battle of Austerlitz in 1805. On December 2, the day of the battle, the sun sets directly in line with the Arc, casting its shadow straight down the Champs-Elysées. And in front of the Arc lies an Unknown Soldier, buried in 1920, two years after the end of the Great War of 1914–18, and commemorated with an eternal flame. It is a remembrance of times past, and a sign that life continues in this great city.

CREDITS

The Automobile Association wishes to thank the following photo libraries for their assistance with the preparation of this project:

Photodisc 49cl

The remaining photographs are held in the Automobile Association's own photo library (**AA World Travel Library**) and were taken by the following photographers:

Martyn Adelman 130bc, 134; **Philip Enticknap** 5bcl, 5bcr, 38bl, 41, 68/9, 95bc, 109r, 112br, 121; **Max Jourdan** 4bl, 4bc, 12/3, 15r, 18cb, 24l, 25, 37, 38bc, 42t, 43tl, 43tr, 46, 47tl, 47tr, 47bl, 47br, 52bl, 52bc, 53t, 53cr, 54l, 55tl, 56bl, 56bc, 57br, 58r, 59r, 60, 60/1, 74l, 74r, 75, 76bc, 78/9, 80/1, 82tr, 83, 86tl, 86r, 87, 88b, 90bl, 90bc, 91tr, 91bl, 95bl, 96l, 97l, 97r, 98tr, 104, 106l, 106r, 107l, 107r, 109bl, 112bc, 119l, 119r, 120tl, 120cr, 123l, 123r, 129, 130br, 132b, 136l, 136br, 137, 138l, 138/9, 139tr, 141r; **Ken Paterson** front cover main, back cover cl, 3cl, 5bl, 14r, 16, 26/7, 33cr, 39bl, 42br, 45, 50, 51r, 76br, 77bl, 81, 82l, 82br, 86bl, 89, 92/3, 94br, 105b, 109tl, 113bl, 113br, 120tr, 120cl, 124, 128, 131bc, 136tr, 141l, 142br; **Betrand Rieger** 14l, 18bl, 21l, 21r, 22cl, 27, 39br, 55bl, 55r, 72, 73t, 77bc, 91tl, 92c, 110tl, 112bl, 113bc, 114/5, 116, 117, 125t, 125b, 126/7; **Clive Sawyer** Back cover cr, r, 3cr, 3r, 6, 10bl, 10br, 11, 17l, 17r, 18br, 19cb, 20, 24r, 28, 29, 30/1, 32tr, 32bl, 33tr, 34/5, 35tr, 35cl, 35cr, 38br, 48/9, 53bl, 54tr, 57bl, 57bc, 58l, 62/3, 66tl, 66tr, 66bl, 66bc, 66br, 67, 70, 71, 73cl, 73cr, 73b, 76bl, 79, 90tc, 91c, 94bl, 94bc, 96r, 98tl, 98cl, 98bl, 98bc, 99tl, 99tr, 99cl, 99bc, 99br, 100tl, 100tr, 100bl, 100bc, 100cr, 101l, 101r, 102, 103, 108, 118, 130bl, 131bl, 132t, 133, 135cl, 140, 142tr; **Barrie Smith** 22tl, 22tr, 23ct, 23bc, 23cr, 32c, 32br; **Tony Souter** Front cover t, Back cover l, 3l, 5br, 19cl, 22cr, 22bl, 23tl, 23tr, 23c, 23bl, 32tl, 33l, 36r, 39bc, 40, 42bl, 43bc, 44, 54br, 59l, 84/5, 88t, 95br, 110tr, 110b, 111l, 111r, 131br, 142l; **James Tims** 8/9, 15l, 51l, 52tl, 52tr, 65, 105t, 122, 143, 144.

If you stand under the Arc de Triomphe and then look up, you'll see this wonderful ceiling decoration.